Trivial Useless and Addictive Information

500 Questions and Answers

Copyright 2021
Chip Trellix

TRIVIAL
Useless and Addictive
Information

500 Questions and Answers

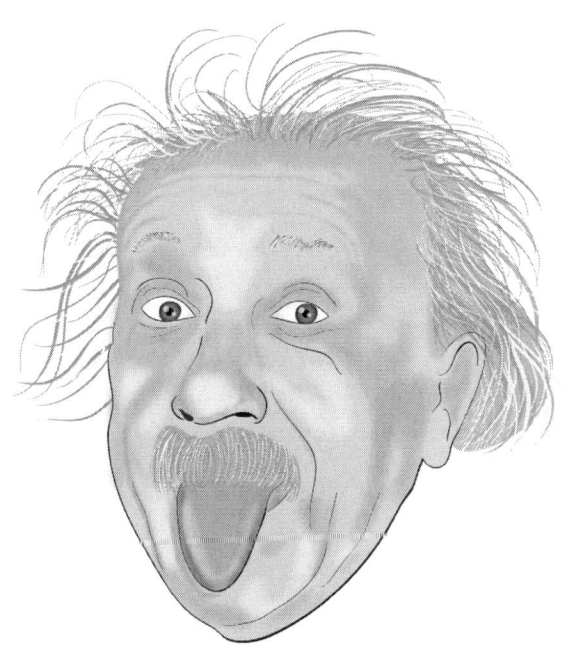

Chip Trellix

1. Who was the first Prime Minister of Canada?

A. John A. Macdonald

B. Robert Borden

C. R. B. Bennett

D. John Abbott

2. Which is the northernmost country?

A. Greenland

B. Mongolia

C. Iceland

D. U.K.

3. Amino acids are the building blocks of which molecules?

A. carbohydrates

B. lipids

C. proteins

D. sugars

4. How many years old is the oldest piece of chewing gum?

A. 2,500 years

B. 11,000 years

C. 9,000 years

D. 6,000 years

5. Who is the only player in NBA history to play 22 seasons?

   A. Robert Parish

   B. Kareem Abdul-Jabbar

   C. Kevin Willis

   D. Vince Carter

6. Power outages in the US are mostly caused by what?

   A. Lightning

   B. Earthquakes

   C. Squirrels

   D. Birds

7. Which franchise has won the most championships in the NBA?

   A. Minneapolis Lakers

   B. Los Angeles Lakers

   C. Boston Celtics

   D. San Antonio Spurs

8. How many sides does home plate have in baseball?

   A. Three

   B. Five

   C. Four

   D. Six

9. Shintoism originated from which country?

   A. India

   B. South Korea

   C. Japan

   D. Thailand

10. Which country has the highest agricultural production?

    A. China

    B. Brazil

    C. Australia

    D. Russia

11. The space between your nostrils is called a what?

    A. A columella

    B. A bridge

    C. A pharange

    D. It doesn't have a name

12. Which is the world's fastest animal on land?

    A. cheetah

    B. leopard

    C. jackrabbit

    D. springbok

13. Which horoscope sign has a crab?

A. Gemini

B. Pisces

C. Scorpio

D. Cancer

14. Which city has the greatest number of museums?

A. Amsterdam

B. Shanghai

C. Stockholm

D. Milan

15. A pangolin is a type of what?

A. amphibian

B. fish

C. mammal

D. reptile

16. What was Harry Houdini's real name?

A. Erik Weisz

B. Aaron Wein

C. Harry Weisz

D. Harry Truman

17. Which country is the biggest?

A. India

B. Japan

C. Thailand

D. Singapore

18. Which planet has the strongest gravitational force?

A. Earth

B. Jupiter

C. Mercury

D. Uranus

19. Which among these countries do NOT use a Peso as its currency?

A. Colombia

B. Philippines

C. Mexico

D. Czech Republic

20. Which is the largest living lizard on earth?

A. crocodile

B. goanna

C. iguana

D. Komodo dragon

21. Yao Ming played for this NBA team:

A. Houston Rockets

B. Golden State Warriors

C. New Orleans Pelicans

D. Atlanta Hawks

22. Which US state has the highest resident population?

A. Texas

B. Ohio

C. California

D. Delaware

23. What is the capital of Romania?

A. Asuncion

B. Belfast

C. Rabat

D. Bucharest

24. Who was the world's first billionaire?

A. Bill Gates

B. Steve Jobs

C. Henry Ford

D. John Rockefeller

25. Which fashion designer was shot dead in the summer of 1997?

   A. Karl Lagerfeld

   B. Oscar de la Renta

   C. Gianni Versace

   D. Ralph Lauren

26. In Minnesota it is illegal to tease what type of animal?

   A. Squirrels

   B. Skunks

   C. Raccoons

   D. Bears

27. Who founded the League of Nations?

   A. Winston Churchill

   B. Mackenzie King

   C. Woodrow Wilson

   D. Jan Smuts

28. Who was the Iron Lady?

   A. Theresa May

   B. Meryl Streep

   C. Margaret Thatcher

   D. Carol Thatcher

29. What does an ornithologist study?

A. birds

B. ears

C. mushrooms

D. organs

30. Who is the leading scorer in NHL history?

A. Stan Mikita

B. Jaromir Jagr

C. Ray Bourque

D. Wayne Gretzky

31. Who is the wife of Zeus?

A. Hera

B. Europa

C. Leda

D. Metis

32. How many games did Ken Griffey Jr. and his father play together?

A. 51

B. 12

C. 2

D. 7

33. What is the official and current name of Big Ben?

A. Clock Tower

B. Bell Tower

C. Elizabeth Tower

D. Victoria Tower

34. Who wrote Flowers for Algernon?

A. Herman Hesse

B. Philip Roth

C. Daniel Keyes

D. Ira Levin

35. What currency is used in South Africa?

A. Dollar

B. Rand

C. Pound

D. Sterling

36. What did Philip II of Macedon lose during battle?

A. Teeth

B. finger

C. ear

D. eye

37. What is the capital city of Canada's Yukon territory?

A. Edmonton

B. Whitehorse

C. Banff

D. Moose Jaw

38. What is the wine capital of the world?

A. Adelaide

B. California

C. Bordeaux

D. Paris

39. What insect has the shortest life span?

A. Fruit Flies

B. Worker Honey Bee

C. Mayflies

D. Spotted Dragonfly

40. What was Veritas the goddess of?

A. Beauty

B. love

C. peace

D. truth

41. How many noses does a slug have?

A. Two

B. Three

C. None

D. Four

42. Which is the oldest geological era?

A. Cenozoic

B. Mesozoic

C. Phanerozoic

D. Precambrian

43. In what country would one compete in a wife carry race?

A. Sweden

B. Denmark

C. Finland

D. Norway

44. Who is the youngest winner in any Grand Slam tournament?

A. Boris Becker

B. Martina Hingis

C. Monica Seles

D. Jennifer Capriati

45. Where is the Sagrada Familia located?

A. Barcelona

B. Madrid

C. Paris

D. Berlin

46. What is Podobromhidrosis?

A. Bad smelling odor from sweat

B. Athlete's foot

C. Unhealthy hair

D. Eyelids that won't open

47. Which dinosaur had 15 horns?

A. Koreaceratops

B. Kosmoceratops

C. Pachyrhinosaurus

D. Protoceratops

48. What is the smallest ocean in the world?

A. The Arctic

B. Indian

C. Mediterranean

D. Southern

49. Which of Shakespeare's plays is the longest?

   A. Macbeth

   B. The Tempest

   C. Hamlet

   D. Taming of the Shrew

50. Which New York Yankee player was nicknamed the "Yankee Clipper"?

   A. Joe DiMaggio

   B. Mickey Mantle

   C. Whitey Ford

   D. Roger Maris

51. Herodotus is considered to be the father of what?

   A. Art

   B. poetry

   C. music

   D. history

52. Suva is the capital of which country?

   A. Estonia

   B. Gabon

   C. Ghana

   D. Fiji

53. How long did the war between England and Zanzibar last?

A. 2 years

B. 3 months

C. 38 minutes

D. 3 hours

54. The traditional Wimbledon colors are green and what?

A. Grey

B. Red Sea

C. Purple

D. Orange

55. Who was the first pope of Rome?

A. Paul

B. John

C. Peter

D. Adam

56. Peaches are the national fruit of which country?

A. Afghanistan

B. Japan

C. Canada

D. Malaysia

57. Where would you find a volcano named Olympus Mons?

A. Greece

B. Pacific Ocean

C. Mars

D. Moon

58. Gladys West is known for her work leading to which invention?

A. computers

B. GPS systems

C. internet

D. x-rays

59. Mt. Everest is located in which country?

A. Nepal

B. USA

C. Canada

D. India

60. What is someone who shoes horses?

A. A ferrier

B. A farrier

C. A farber

D. A harrier

61. What is the second largest French-speaking city in the world?

A. Abidjan

B. Montreal

C. Dakar

D. Port-au-Prince

62. What is a baby goat called?

A. A kid

B. A pup

C. A child

D. A goatling

63. Who invented the rocking chair?

A. Thomas Edison

B. Nikola Tesla

C. Thomas Jefferson

D. Benjamin Franklin

64. What is the capital of Qatar?

A. Dukhan

B. Doha

C. Abu Dhabi

D. Dubai

65. Which part of the brain interprets light and color?

A. frontal lobe

B. parietal lobe

C. occipital lobe

D. temporal lobe

66. A flamboyance is a group of what animals?

A. Doves

B. Dolphins

C. Geese

D. Flamingos

67. A light year is a measure of what?

A. acceleration

B. distance

C. speed

D. time

68. What is the most spoken language?

A. Mandarin

B. French

C. English

D. Spanish

69. Which atmospheric layer is closest to the earth's surface?

   A. exosphere

   B. mesosphere

   C. stratosphere

   D. troposphere

70. Charles Darwin is famous for the theory of what?

   A. continental drift

   B. evolution

   C. relativity

   D. the big bang

71. Europe is separated from Africa by which sea?

   A. Mediterranean Sea

   B. Black Sea

   C. Red Sea

   D. Balkan Sea

72. What was Cleopatra's nationality?

   A. Mesopotamian

   B. Greek. Egyptian

   C. Macedonian

   D. Macedonian

73. From which language did the word Ketchup come?

   A. French

   B. Aztec

   C. Chinese

   D. Hindi

74. Who was Catherine the Great's husband?

   A. Ivan I

   B. Peter III

   C. Paul I

   D. Peter II

75. The aardvark is native to which continent?

   A. Asia

   B. South America

   C. Oceania

   D. Africa

76. What planets literally rain diamonds?

   A. Uranus and Neptune

   B. Mercury and Venus

   C. Saturn and Neptune

   D. Saturn and Jupiter

77. What was Ho Chi Minh city originally called?

A. Saigon

B. Laos

C. Hanoi

D. Hue

78. A joule is a measurement of what?

A. energy

B. force

C. mass

D. speed

79. Adobo is a dish that originated from which country?

A. Thailand

B. Spain

C. Portugal

D. Philippines

80. Which US state has the longest cave system in the world?

A. Tennessee

B. Arizona

C. Virginia

D. Kentucky

81. What country was formerly referred to as Persia?

　A. Egypt

　B. Iran

　C. Greece

　D. Italy

82. Which King of England broke apart from the Catholic Church?

　A. John

　B. Henry VIII

　C. Charles II

　D. George

83. How many hearts does an octopus have?

　A. Four

　B. Three

　C. Two

　D. Six

84. In which state will you find Mount Rushmore?

　A. Tennessee

　B. South Dakota

　C. Connecticut

　D. Vermont

85. Which among these cities is NOT a capital?

A. Pyongyang

B. Amsterdam

C. Manila

D. Toronto

86. How many Theses did Martine Luther write?

A. 99

B. 100

C. 90

D. 95

87. What is allspice alternatively known as?

A. Garlic

B. Pimento

C. Saffron

D. Thyme

88. Which U.S. President served 3 terms?

A. Roosevelt

B. Washington

C. Carter

D. Adams

89. Which U.S. President was the first to hold a Patent?

A. Washington

B. Adams

C. Jackson

D. Lincoln

90. British Tanks have the equipment to make which beverage?

A. Coffee

B. beer

C. tea

D. wine

91. The album Bleach was the debut studio album by what rock band?

A. Nirvana

B. Green Day

C. Red Hot Chili Peppers

D. Pearl Jam

92. Which Germany Official ordered the Final Solution?

A. Hitler

B. Goering

C. Himmler

D. Heydrich

93. Marilyn Monroe was married to which famous sportsman?

A. Yogi Berra

B. Justin Verlander

C. Ralph Kiner

D. Joe DiMaggio

94. What animal is constitutionally protected in Florida?

A. Alligators

B. Deer

C. Ducks

D. Pigs

95. The smallest state in the US is?

A. Rhode Island

B. Delaware

C. North Dakota

D. South Dakota

96. What was the first fruit that was eaten on the moon?

A. Apple

B. Plum

C. Melon

D. Peach

97. In which of Britney's video does she appear as a stewardess?

   A. Baby One More Time

   B. Womanizer

   C. Toxic

   D. Pretty Girls

98. Which animal was the first animal in space?

   A. Fruit flies

   B. dogs

   C. monkeys

   D. cats

99. What color is Absinthe?

   A. Orange

   B. Green

   C. Blue

   D. White

100. As what type of beans are chickpeas also known as?

   A. Great White North

   B. Pinto

   C. Black

   D. Garbanzo

101. Which Dutch artist painted Girl with a Pearl Earring?

A. Rembrandt

B. Mondrian

C. Vermeer

D. Bosch

102. In 1947 Britain granted Independence to which nation?

A. China

B. India

C. Australia

D. Canada

103. Which gas makes the bubbles in a soda drink?

A. argon

B. carbon dioxide

C. nitrogen

D. oxygen

104. In 1979 the USSR invaded which country?

A. China

B. Iran

C. Afghanistan

D. Ukraine

105. How many states are there in the USA?

A. 60

B. 50

C. 32

D. 49

106. How many French Open titles has Rafael Nadal won?

A. 10

B. 8

C. 12

D. 13

107. Which country is the least populated?

A. Vatican City

B. Palau

C. Monaco

D. San Marino

108. Martin Luther sparked which event?

A. French Revolution

B. Crimean War

C. Protestant Reformation

D. WWI

109. What is the capital of Australia's Northern Territory?

A. Darwin

B. Katherine

C. Tennant Creek

D. Alice Springs

110. Which gas makes up 91% of the sun?

A. helium

B. hydrogen

C. nitrogen

D. oxygen

111. Which River flows through the Grand Canyon?

A. Colorado River

B. Missouri River

C. Yukon River

D. Rio Grande

112. Which NFL team draws its name from a poem by Edgar Allan Poe?

A. Chicago Bears

B. Baltimore Ravens

C. New England Patriots

D. Pittsburgh Steelers

113. What is the longest river?

A. Yellow River

B. Congo River

C. Nile

D. Mekong River

114. What is the main component of Saturn's rings?

A. dust

B. gas

C. ice

D. rock

115. What was the name of the ship that Charles Darwin sailed on?

A. Beagle

B. Endeavour

C. Golden Hind

D. Victory

116. In Georgia, it is illegal to eat what with a fork?

A. Macaroni

B. Potato salad

C. Fried chicken

D. Okra

117. What color does gold leaf appear if you hold it up to the light?

A. Blue

B. Green

C. Violet

D. Amber

118. Carrots are a good source of which vitamin?

A. Vitamin C

B. Vitamin B

C. Vitamin E

D. Vitamin A

119. Which country is known as the Land of White Elephant?

A. India

B. Thailand

C. Cambodia

D. Vietnam

120. Madras is now called as which Indian city?

A. Chennai

B. Kolkata

C. Jaipur

D. Surat

121. What is the process of a liquid changing to a gas called?

A. condensation

B. evaporation

C. melting

D. sublimation

122. Who was childhood friends with Harper Lee?

A. George Orwell

B. Truman Capote

C. Louisa Alcott

D. Jane Austen

123. What color is a polar bear's skin?

A. Black

B. Brown

C. White

D. Spotted

124. What country won the Eurovision Song Contest 2017?

A. Spain

B. Portugal

C. Croatia

D. Sweden

125. Which of these states is in the West Coast?

  A. New York

  B. California

  C. Virginia

  D. Rhode Island

126. Which of these numbers is larger?

  A. billion

  B. centillion

  C. googol

  D. trillion

127. What is the most common letter in the English alphabet?

  A. S

  B. A collection

  C. E

  D. The moon

128. Which chess piece can only move diagonally?

  A. Pawn

  B. Rook

  C. Bishop

  D. Horse

129. What was France originally called?

A. Gaul

B. Lutetia

C. Lyon

D. Merea

130. What of these animals is not an amphibian?

A. eel

B. frog

C. salamander

D. toad

131. In what city is The Parthenon located?

A. Patras

B. Kavala

C. Volos

D. Athens

132. Fidel Castro was the leader of which country?

A. Porto Rico

B. Mexico

C. Brazil

D. Cuba

133. In what field did Marie Curie work?

A. astronomy

B. physics

C. geology

D. radioactivity

134. Pol Pot ruled which country from 1975-1979?

A. India

B. China

C. Cambodia

D. Vietnam

135. Which U.S. state held the first Black Women's Rights Convention?

A. New York

B. Ohio

C. Michigan

D. Illinois

136. Which dynasty build most of the Great Wall of China?

A. Shang

B. Zhou

C. Ming

D. Yuan

137. Who gifted the Statue of Liberty to the U.S.?

  A. England

  B. Canada

  C. France

  D. Italy

138. Who voices Morty in the series Rick and Morty?

  A. Robert Redford

  B. Gray Jackson

  C. Justin Rolland

  D. Toni Scarroli

139. What is the hallux?

  A. Big toe

  B. Pinky finger

  C. Collarbone

  D. First rib

140. How would you write the number 54 in roman numerals?

  A. LIV

  B. LVI

  C. XXXXIV

  D. XXXXIIII

141. What currency started in issuing in 2002?

A. Euro

B. Yen

C. Franc

D. Ruble

142. What was Babe Ruth's first name?

A. George

B. Gregory

C. Gerald

D. Gary

143. Who was the first U.S Secretary of Treasury?

A. Alexander Hamilton

B. John Adams

C. Aaron Burr

D. Thomas Edison

144. Which country has never lost a war?

A. Pakistan

B. North Korea

C. Israel

D. USA

145. Which country has the most number of pets per household?

   A. USA

   B. New Zealand

   C. Bhutan

   D. India

146. Who discovered King Tut's tomb?

   A. Henry Wilson

   B. Howard Carter

   C. Charles Smith

   D. Edward Peters

147. What does BMW stand for (in English)?

   A. British Motor Works

   B. Bavarian Motor Works

   C. Belgium Motor Works

   D. Berlin Motor Works

148. Which is the youngest country?

   A. Senegal

   B. San Marino

   C. Ethiopia

   D. Timor-Leste

149. Which date was Julius Caesar killed?

A. March 15th

B. March 30th

C. February 15th

D. March 17th

150. Which country invented paper?

A. China

B. Japan

C. USA

D. Spain

151. In what year was the first iPhone released?

A. 2005

B. 2007

C. 2009

D. 2010

152. What was the famous Roe vs. Wade case about?

A. Slavery

B. drugs

C. abortion

D. same-sex marriage

153. By which nickname were Stephen Curry and Klay Thompson known as?

A. Bruise Brothers

B. Splash Brothers

C. Twin Towers

D. Death Lineup

154. Joan of Arc is which of the following?

A. Criminal

B. witch

C. saint

D. hero

155. Which country consumes the most chocolate per capita?

A. USA

B. France

C. Switzerland

D. Germany

156. What happened in the Soviet Union from 1933-1934?

A. Famine

B. War

C. Uprising

D. Political conflicts

157. Which golfing legend was nicknamed The King?

A. Tiger Woods

B. Arnold Palmer

C. Jack Nicklaus

D. Gary Player

158. Who invented scissors?

A. Hero of Alexander

B. Leonardo da Vinci

C. Johannes Guttenberg

D. Hans Janssen

159. What is the capital of Australia?

A. Sydney

B. Canberra

C. Melbourne

D. Brisbane

160. What country has the world's most ancient forest?

A. Germany

B. Canada

C. China

D. Australia

161. What is the smallest country in the world?

A. Monaco

B. Liechtenstein

C. Malta

D. Vatican City

162. Which of the following is not considered to be a greenhouse gas?

A. carbon dioxide

B. methane

C. oxygen

D. water vapor

163. Who was the first Tudor Monarch in England?

A. Henry VII

B. Victoria

C. Elizabeth

D. George III

164. Canberra is the capital city of which country?

A. New Zealand

B. Australia

C. Papua New Guinea

D. Fiji

165. Who played Cher Horowitz in the movie Clueless?

A. Alicia Silverstone

B. Stacey Dash

C. Brittany Murphy

D. Uma Thurman

166. The Burj Khalifa is located in which country?

A. UAE

B. South Sudan

C. Oman

D. Saudi Arabia

167. What is the chemical symbol for silver?

A. Ag

B. Au

C. Si

D. Sr

168. What was the Titanic's official job?

A. Deliver mail

B. passenger liner

C. cargo ship

D. carry animals

169. Which bird has the largest wingspan of any living bird?

   A. The Great Red Hawk

   B. Blakiston's Fish Owl

   C. The wandering Albatross

   D. Andean Condor

170. What year did Harriet Tubman escape slavery?

   A. 1850

   B. 1845

   C. 1849

   D. 1840

171. Which country uses the most renewable energy?

   A. Iceland

   B. Spain

   C. Ireland

   D. Finland

172. Humans have 7 neck vertebrae. How many do giraffes have?

   A. 4

   B. 7

   C. 10

   D. 14

173. What is the longest river in Australia?

A. The Murray River

B. The Darling River

C. Lachlan River

D. Cooper Creek

174. Carbohydrates are made up of which unit molecules?

A. amino acids

B. lipids

C. proteins

D. sugars

175. Where on the human body is the zygomatic bone found?

A. Eyebrow

B. Pelvis

C. Facial cheek

D. Foot

176. What is the outermost layer of the earth called?

A. asthenosphere

B. lithosphere

C. mesosphere

D. outer core

177. What was the ice cream cone invented for?

A. To hold pens

B. To use in bowling

C. To hold flowers

D. To eat by itself

178. Tanks were used in battle for the first time in which conflict?

A. War of 1912

B. Russian Revolution

C. World War 2

D. World War 1

179. Which is the closest star to earth

A. Alpha Centauri

B. Proxima Centauri

C. Sirius

D. Sun

180. How long is New Zealand's Ninety Mile Beach?

A. 91 miles

B. 64 miles

C. 45 miles

D. 55 miles

181. Which country was the first to use flamethrowers in WWI?

A. France

B. England

C. Russia

D. Germany

182. NFL player Dick Plasman is famous for:

A. Inventing the huddle

B. A 99-yard touchdown pass

C. Last player to play without a helmet

D. Played in both MLB and NFL

183. Dorothy Hodgkin won a Nobel Prize for her work in which subject?

A. astronomy

B. genetics

C. geology

D. x-ray crystallography

184. What is secreted from the lacrimal gland?

A. adrenaline

B. saliva

C. sweat

D. tears

185. Which among these records does Magic Johnson hold?

A. Oldest player to score 30+ points in a game

B. Oldest player to score 50+ points in a game

C. Oldest player to score 40+ points in a game

D. Youngest to score 50+ points in a game

186. What's the best known artificial international language?

A. Esperanto

B. Esperanzo

C. Elfin

D. Elven

187. Which country is predominantly atheist?

A. China

B. Algeria

C. India

D. Bangladesh

188. Taylor Swift grew up on what type of farm?

A. Christmas Tree Farm

B. Peanut Farm

C. Corn Farm

D. Potato Farm

189. Which two countries are connected by the Karakoram Pass?

A. China and Nepal

B. Pakistan and Afghanistan

C. China and Russia

D. China and India

190. What year was the internet founded?

A. 1980

B. 1990

C. 1989

D. 1988

191. Which country was the first to use paper currency?

A. England

B. France

C. China

D. India

192. The Augusta National Golf Club is located in which U.S. State?

A. South Carolina

B. Georgia

C. Florida

D. North Carolina

193. What is the fungi Hydnellum Peckii also known as?

A. Blood cap

B. Black mold

C. The golden crown fungus

D. The bleeding tooth fungus

194. King Henry VI of England was also the king of which country?

A. Spain

B. Italy

C. France

D. Russia

195. What did the Olympics used to award medals for?

A. Art

B. Singing

C. Writing

D. Speaking

196. Which element has the symbol Pb?

A. gold

B. lead

C. potassium

D. phosphorus

197. What year did Canada become a country?

A. 1867

B. 1870

C. 1890

D. 1857

198. What is the most abundant element in the universe?

A. Hydrogen

B. Oxygen

C. Carbon

D. Neon

199. What did Alexander Graham Bell invent?

A. doorbell

B. lightbulb

C. telephone

D. television

200. How many times did Richard Petty win the Daytona 500?

A. 11

B. 12

C. 9

D. 7

201. Which city is the most sung about?

A. New York

B. Miami

C. Los Angeles

D. London

202. What country was formerly called Ceylon?

A. Tanzania

B. Sri Lanka

C. Haiti

D. Canada

203. Which is the smallest organ in the human body?

A. appendix

B. gall bladder

C. pineal gland

D. spleen

204. Caravaggio shared a first name with what other famous artist?

A. Claude

B. Giorgio

C. Raphael

D. Michelangelo

205. How many countries have names that end in -stan?

A. 10

B. 5

C. 8

D. 7

206. Where in your body is your axilla?

A. ankle

B. armpit

C. ear

D. knee

207. Which author's last words were I want nothing but death?

A. Mark Twain

B. Jane Austen

C. Louisa Alcott

D. Mary Shelley

208. In 1789 where did the French Third Estate take their oath?

A. Bastille

B. courthouse

C. tennis court

D. theater

209. Who is the oldest player ever to hit 500 home runs?

A. Ted Williams

B. Gary Sheffield

C. Mel Ott

D. Willie Mays

210. Who painted the Mona Lisa?

A. Michelangelo

B. Leonardo da Vinci

C. Edgar Degas

D. Raphael

211. How has the Statue of Liberty changed since it was built?

A. It was moved to a new location

B. It changed color

C. Features were added

D. The original flame collapsed

212. Which country has the highest number of tourists yearly?

A. Japan

B. France

C. Thailand

D. Greece

213. Where is the Easter Island located?

A. Chile

B. China

C. Morocco

D. Singapore

214. The world's largest theme park is located in which country?

A. USA

B. Japan

C. France

D. Brazil

215. What is the real first name of Marilyn Monroe?

A. Norma Jeane

B. Grace Reed

C. Daisy Wilder

D. Regina Mack

216. Which is the biggest moon in the solar system?

A. Ganymede (Jupiter)

B. Io (Jupiter)

C. Moon (Earth)

D. Titan (Saturn)

217. How many US states begin with the letter A?

A. 4

B. 5

C. 8

D. 2

218. Biscuit is roughly translated to mean what?

A. Fluffy puck

B. Twice cooked

C. Once cooked

D. Soft circle

219. Who did Aaron Burr kill?

A. Abraham Lincoln

B. Alexander Hamilton

C. George Washington

D. Thomas Jefferson

220. Nairobi is the capital of which country?

A. Kenya

B. Ukraine

C. Libya

D. Guatemala

221. How many vaginas do kangaroos have?

A. One

B. Two

C. Three

D. Four

222. Which is the longest bone in the human body?

A. femur

B. fibula

C. sternum

D. tibia

223. Which was the largest tank battle in history?

A. Somme

B. Britain

C. Kursk

D. Stalingrad

224. Outside which New York building was John Lennon killed?

A. Chrysler Building

B. Museum of Modern Art

C. The Dakota

D. The Guggenheim

225. Other than a General what was Stonewall Jackson's other career?

A. Carpentry

B. lawyer

C. teacher

D. merchant

226. In which year did President Jimmy Carter file a UFO report?

A. 1973

B. 1975

C. 1980

D. 1970

227. Who is the only non-American to win all four majors in a career?

A. Bernhard Langer

B. Vijay Singh

C. Gary Player

D. Sergio Garcia

228. Which of these elements is not a metal?

A. mercury

B. neon

C. sodium

D. tungsten

229. Galileo was the citizen of which country?

A. France

B. Portugal

C. Italy

D. Germany

230. Who established the 365-day calendar?

A. Augustus

B. Julius Caesar

C. Trajan

D. Henry VI

231. What does the R stand for on the rating of a movie?

A. Registered

B. Restricted

C. Rap

D. Regulated

232. Osteoporosis is a disease affecting which part of the body?

A. blood

B. bones

C. brain

D. skin

233. In which city was Anne Frank's hiding place?

A. Amsterdam

B. Paris

C. London

D. Brussels

234. Which city is shared by two countries?

A. Luxembourg

B. Seville

C. Granada

D. Marseille

235. What kind of animal is a bustard?

A. A bird

B. A toad

C. A skunk

D. A lizard

236. What is Bob Dylan's real name?

A. Lind Zimmerman

B. Robert Zimmerman

C. Adam Zimmerman

D. Jonathan Zimmerman

237. The kiwi is native to which country?

A. Australia

B. Solomon Islands

C. New Zealand

D. Fiji

238. How many stars make up the constellation known as Orion's Belt?

A. 2

B. 3

C. 4

D. 5

239. In which U.S. state was the atomic bomb tested in?

A. New York

B. New Mexico

C. Nevada

D. Texas

240. How many time zones are in Florida?

A. 2

B. 1

C. 5

D. 3

241. What did Harriet Tubman suffer from as a child?

A. Head injury

B. smallpox

C. influenza

D. leg injury

242. In which country is the Trois-Rivieres bridge?

A. France

B. Canada

C. Vietnam

D. Algeria

243. Which animal kills the most people worldwide?

A. dog

B. mosquito

C. shark

D. snake

244. What is the capital of South Korea?

A. Busan

B. Jeju

C. Daegu

D. Seoul

245. What was major league baseball's Yogi Berra's real name?

A. Yogi Berrarand

B. Peter Berra

C. Yogi Johnson

D. Lawrence Peter Berra

246. What did J. Edgar Hoover not want people walking on?

A. His legacy

B. His dropped cigarette butts

C. His words

D. His shadow

247. New York City comprises how many boroughs?

A. 4

B. 6

C. 3

D. 5

248. What is dendrochronology?

A. climate science

B. study of skin

C. study of teeth

D. tree-ring dating

249. What flavor is Cointreau?

A. Lime

B. Lemon

C. Orange

D. Grapefruit

250. Which city has the busiest airport in the world?

A. California

B. London

C. Singapore

D. Atlanta

251. How long does it take for light from the sun to reach the earth?

A. 2 seconds

B. 8 seconds

C. 8 minutes

D. 20 minutes

252. In which branch of the arts is Katherine Dunham famous?

A. Interpretive Dance

B. Tap dancing

C. Performance Arts

D. Ballet

253. Where would you find the Yangtze River?

   A. India

   B. China

   C. Indonesia

   D. Papua New Guinea

254. Where did Rene Descartes spend the last year of his life?

   A. France

   B. Belgium

   C. Sweden

   D. Denmark

255. Which among these countries do not use the metric system?

   A. England

   B. Liberia

   C. Germany

   D. South Sudan

256. The Warren Spahn Award is given to:

   A. Best left-handed pitcher

   B. Most outstanding designated hitter

   C. Best pitcher of the season

   D. Top hitter in each league

257. Which country offered Albert Einstein presidency?

A. Germany

B. Austria

C. Israel

D. Poland

258. Which planet is the hottest in the solar system?

A. Venus

B. Mercury

C. Jupiter

D. Mars

259. Which Roman Emperor liked to fight in games?

A. Commodus

B. Trajan

C. Titus

D. Caligula

260. Port-au-Prince is the capital of which country?

A. Dominican Republic

B. Haiti

C. Suriname

D. Grenada

261. What country was formerly called Siam?

A. Laos

B. Indonesia

C. Iran

D. Thailand

262. What is the most linguistically diverse country in the world?

A. Papua New Guinea

B. USA

C. Australia

D. Ireland

263. Which two U.S. states do not observe Daylight Saving Time?

A. Arizona and New Mexico

B. Arizona and Hawaii

C. Texas and North Dakota

D. Hawaii and California

264. What is the most populous city in Canada?

A. Vancouver

B. Toronto

C. Montreal

D. Quebec City

265. What kind of animal is a firefly?

A. Fly

B. Beetle

C. Moth

D. Bee

266. Who wrote To Kill a Mockingbird?

A. Harper Lee

B. Margaret Atwood

C. Jane Austen

D. Louisa Alcott

267. What is the capital of Finland?

A. Oslo

B. Oulu

C. Vaasa

D. Helsinki

268. An ohm is a measure of what?

A. current

B. power

C. resistance

D. voltage

269. In June in Wyoming, it is illegal to take a picture of what?

A. An elk

B. A bison

C. A geyser

D. A rabbit

270. What is the unit of electrical current?

A. amp

B. ohm

C. volt

D. watt

271. Which of these items was not invented by Leonardo da Vinci?

A. bicycle

B. diving suit

C. helicopter

D. parachute

272. Which River flows through Paris?

A. River Seine

B. Moon River

C. River Thames

D. Yellow River

273. Which US state is also called the Aloha State?

A. Hawaii

B. Arizona

C. Colorado

D. Delaware

274. What was Toyota's first popular hybrid car called?

A. Yaris

B. Matrix

C. Prius

D. Camry

275. What igneous rock has a density less than water?

A. Basalt

B. Granite

C. Scoria

D. Pumice

276. How many ribs are in a human body?

A. 16

B. 28

C. 22

D. 24

277. In regard to data storage what does the acronym SSD stand for?

A. Solid State Drive

B. Standard Sorting Device

C. Storage Sorting Drive

D. Solid Storage Data

278. In which city is the White House located?

A. New York

B. San Francisco

C. Los Angeles

D. Washington D.C.

279. How many countries are part of Great Britain?

A. 3

B. 4

C. 5

D. 2

280. Which is the longest NASCAR oval?

A. El Dorado Speedway

B. Daytona International Speedway

C. Talladega Superspeedway

D. Phoenix Raceway

281. Which country was Joseph Stalin born in?

A. Georgia

B. Ukraine

C. Russia

D. Serbia

282. Which country has the most mountains?

A. India

B. USA

C. China

D. Russia

283. Which Roman Emperor made his horse a Senator?

A. Caesar

B. Augustus

C. Brutus

D. Caligula

284. What is the hardest substance in the human body?

A. bone

B. tooth enamel

C. fingernail

D. toenail

285. Who wrote Frankenstein?

A. Mary Shelley

B. Percy Shelley

C. Franklin Stein

D. Howard Young

286. Who was the first person to suggest Daylight Savings Times?

A. Benjamin Franklin

B. Adam Smith

C. George Washington

D. Thomas Jefferson

287. Who was the first mascot of the Cincinnati Reds baseball team?

A. Mr. Redlegs

B. Mr. Red

C. Gapper

D. Paws

288. Who plays the role of Lou Gehrig in the Pride of the Yankees?

A. Gary Cooper

B. Robert Redford

C. Walter Brennan

D. Ernie Adams

289. Where were the fortune cookies invented?

A. San Francisco

B. Shanghai

C. Tokyo

D. Busan

290. What was the Louvre in Paris before it became a museum?

A. Government Building

B. Courthouse

C. Palace

D. University

291. Where did the first hot air Balloon ride take place?

A. Berlin

B. Paris

C. London

D. Madrid

292. What is the mass of 1 liter of water?

A. 100 grams

B. 1 kilogram

C. 1 pint

D. 1 pound

293. Who was the first Time Magazine Man of the Year?

A. Henry Ford

B. Winston Churchill

C. Harry Truman

D. Charles Lindbergh

294. Florence Nightingale aided the sick and wounded during what war

A. The Boer Wars

B. The War of 1812

C. The Crimean War

D. The Revolutionary War

295. How many countries border China?

A. 10

B. 8

C. 14

D. 19

296. Which is considered the coffee capital of the world?

A. Seoul

B. Wellington

C. Melbourne

D. Vienna

297. What is the painting La Gioconda more usually known as?

   A. Mona Lisa

   B. Girl with a Pearl Earring

   C. The Starry Night

   D. The Scream

298. Which Philosopher tutored Alexander the Great?

   A. Plato

   B. Isocrates

   C. Ptolemy

   D. Aristotle

299. Who was the cartoonist behind the Far Side Gallery?

   A. Scott Adams

   B. Robert Crumb

   C. Gary Larson

   D. Walt Disney

300. What is the biggest artery in the human body?

   A. Femoral

   B. Aorta

   C. Coronary

   D. Left Anterior Descending

301. Where was the telescope invented?

A. England

B. Germany

C. Italy

D. Japan

302. What Island state was formerly known by the name Formosa?

A. Taiwan

B. The Philippines

C. New Zealand

D. Japan

303. What is the softest mineral in the world?

A. Diamond

B. Calcite

C. Talc

D. Apatite

304. What is the state capital of New York?

A. New York City

B. Albany

C. Rochester

D. Utica

305. Which of the following is a nautical unit for speed?

A. cable

B. fathom

C. knot

D. nautical mile

306. What book starts with the line Call me Ishmael??

A. Brave New World

B. The Plague

C. 100 Years of Solitude

D. Moby Dick

307. How many elements are in the period table?

A. 98

B. 103

C. 112

D. 118

308. What is the smallest country in the world?

A. Liechtenstein

B. Marshall Islands

C. Vatican City

D. Monaco

309. Which color has the highest frequency in the visible spectrum?

A. blue

B. indigo

C. red

D. violet

310. What is the Higgs boson?

A. element

B. molecule

C. subatomic particle

D. theory of gravity

311. The Saffir-Simpson scale measures the intensity of what?

A. earthquakes

B. hailstorm

C. hurricanes

D. waves

312. What is the most abundant metal in the Earth's crust?

A. Iron

B. Lead

C. Aluminum

D. Sodium

313. Who created the animated series Futurama?

A. Homer Groening

B. John Groening

C. Adam Groening

D. Matt Groening

314. Where do kiwi fruits originally come from?

A. Taiwan

B. Vietnam

C. China

D. India

315. Who claimed he could drive away the devil with a fart?

A. Pope Pius X

B. King Louis IX

C. Martin Luther

D. Napoleon

316. What was the first law code called?

A. Code of Ur-Nammu

B. 12 tables

C. Code of Sargon

D. Code of Hammurabi

317. In electricity - what does the abbreviation AC stand for?

A. alternating circuit

B. alternating charge

C. alternating current

D. alternative current

318. How many time zones does the United States have?

A. 12

B. 9

C. 5

D. 14

319. Which country has three capital cities?

A. Yemen

B. Sri Lanka

C. South Africa

D. Russia

320. What type of business did Annie have that failed in Bridesmaids?

A. Bakery

B. Tailor

C. Cafe

D. Florist

321. Which U.S. state has Garden State as its nickname?

A. New York

B. New Jersey

C. Connecticut

D. Rhode Island

322. Which Ocean is the Bermuda Triangle located?

A. North Atlantic

B. Pacific

C. Indian

D. Arctic

323. Who wrote Around the World in 80 Days?

A. Jules Verne

B. Herman Melville

C. Tom Clancy

D. Bram Stoker

324. Which basketball player appeared in the 2015 film Trainwreck?

A. LeBron James

B. Wilt Chamberlain

C. Kevin Durant

D. Michael Jordan

325. What is the common name for enuresis?

A. Bedwetting

B. Hot flashes

C. Fever

D. Runny nose

326. Where was the first tank produced?

A. England

B. France

C. Germany

D. the U.S.

327. Which country did Germany invade first in WWII?

A. France

B. Belgium

C. Poland

D. Romania

328. What is the currency of Japan?

A. yen

B. won

C. dollar

D. krone

329. What is the capital city of Paraguay?

A. Concepcion

B. Tarija

C. Rosario

D. Asuncion

330. Who organized the Boston Tea Party in 1773?

A. Samuel Adams

B. John Adams

C. Aaron Burr

D. John Cook

331. Which creatures produce gossamer?

A. Silkworms

B. A spider

C. Moths

D. Caterpillars

332. Name the only New York Yankee to hit four home runs in one game?

A. Ty Cobb

B. Joe DiMaggio

C. Micky Mantle

D. Lou Gehrig

333. What is Harry Potter's Patronus?

A. A stag

B. A raven

C. A cat

D. A hawk

334. Platypuses are endemic to which county?

A. Australia

B. Ecuador

C. Brazil

D. USA

335. Where did Heineken beer originate?

A. Germany

B. Belgium

C. The Netherlands

D. Denmark

336. Where was Alexander Graham Bell born?

A. England

B. Ireland

C. Scotland

D. France

337. What does a Scoville unit measure?

A. Acidity

B. Aroma

C. Spiciness

D. Heat

338. In Swedish a skvader is a rabbit with what unusual feature?

A. Wings

B. Canine teeth

C. Blue eyes

D. No tail

339. The Mayans worshiped which animal as gods?

A. Horses

B. cats

C. rabbits

D. turkeys

340. Which among these countries is located in two continents?

A. Sweden

B. Switzerland

C. Turkey

D. China

341. Which war did George Orwell fight in?

A. WWI

B. WWII

C. the Spanish Civil war

D. the Russian Civil War

342. Which country is considered as land locked?

A. Greenland

B. Kazakhstan

C. Portugal

D. Pakistan

343. What year did women get the right to vote in the U.S?

A. 1920

B. 1919

C. 1918

D. 1921

344. Which of these substances is acidic?

A. ammonia

B. limewater

C. soap

D. vinegar

345. The Sudanese Republic is now which country?

A. Mali

B. Guinea

C. Ghana

D. South Sudan

346. How would you write the number 5 in binary code?

A. 1

B. 11

C. 101

D. 111

347. Pope Gregory IX believed which animal aided devil worship?

A. Cats

B. dogs

C. owls

D. rabbits

348. Where is the Machu Picchu located?

A. Nepal

B. Brazil

C. Peru

D. Myanmar

349. A cross appears in the flags of these countries except:

A. Tonga

B. Georgia

C. Switzerland

D. Spain

350. What was the first name of the first American born saint?

A. Anne

B. Martha

C. Elizabeth

D. Paul

351. Where was Alexander Hamilton born?

A. America

B. France

C. Nevis

D. Cuba

352. Where is the Stone Henge located?

A. England

B. Netherlands

C. Pakistan

D. Brazil

353. Who introduced the world's first mass-produced car?

A. Louis Chevrolet

B. Walter Chrysler

C. Henry Ford

D. William Durant

354. How many moons does the planet Venus have?

A. 0

B. 1

C. 2

D. 12

355. The longest cave system is located in which country?

A. Russia

B. USA

C. China

D. India

356. What was the predecessor to the United Nations?

A. Association of Nations

B. League of Nations

C. League of Empires

D. the Allied Nations

357. What was the name of the first satellite launched into space?

A. Atlas

B. Apollo I

C. Mir

D. Sputnik I

358. Who was the captain of the Titanic?

A. Robert Fields

B. J. Bruce Ismay

C. Alexander Carlisle

D. Edward Smith

359. Mount Kilimanjaro is located in which country?

A. Tanzania

B. India

C. USA

D. Poland

360. Which of these is not a type of quark?

A. charm

B. down

C. round

D. up

361. Who was monarch after Queen Elizabeth I?

A. Henry VI

B. George II

C. Victoria

D. James VI

362. In Minnesota it is illegal to be what in bed?

A. Sweating

B. Singing

C. Naked

D. Wearing hiking boots

363. What is a haboob?

A. A type of savory pie

B. A type of sandstorm

C. A type of bird

D. A person who forgets things

364. Where was the world's smallest fish discovered?

A. Indonesia

B. Brazil

C. Australia

D. Turkey

365. What was the name of Alexander the Great's horse?

A. Alexander II

B. Achilles

C. Bucephalus

D. Patrocles

366. Where did the Battle of Stalingrad take place?

A. Germany

B. Soviet Union

C. Poland

D. France

367. What is the only bird known to fly backwards?

A. Sparrow

B. Hummingbird

C. Cape Teal

D. White Headed Petril

368. What city did Starbucks open its first store in 1971?

A. Tacoma

B. San Francisco

C. Portland

D. Seattle

369. What country has competitive office chair racing?

A. Thailand

B. Japan

C. Chile

D. Canada

370. In what year did Neil Armstrong land on the moon?

A. 1966

B. 1967

C. 1968

D. 1969

371. Which is the longer distance?

A. 1 furlong

B. 1 kilometer

C. 1 mile

D. 1 yard

372. What religion did Joseph Smith form?

A. Christianity

B. Mormonism

C. Judaism

D. New Thought Movement

373. Abbey Road is located in which city?

A. Leeds

B. Nottingham

C. London

D. Bristol

374. What is the longest English word with only one vowel?

A. Tally

B. Strengths

C. Twelve

D. Lovely

375. What is the tallest breed of dog in the world?

A. Scottish Deerhound

B. The Great Dane

C. Saint Bernard

D. English Mastiff

376. Which continent is in all four hemispheres?

A. Africa

B. Asia

C. Antarctica

D. Europe

377. Where would you find cellulose?

A. blood cells

B. plant tissue

C. rocks

D. space

378. Where is the Sea of Tranquility located?

A. Mars

B. Earth

C. Jupiter

D. The moon

379. Which president is responsible for the forward pass?

A. William Howard Taft

B. William McKinley

C. Teddy Roosevelt

D. Franklin D. Roosevelt

380. What was J. Edgar Hoover the director of?

A. CIA

B. Homeland Security

C. FBI

D. U.S. Army

381. How did Marie Antoinette die?

A. Accident

B. drowning

C. illness

D. beheaded

382. Which of these elements are not found in the structure of DNA?

A. calcium

B. carbon

C. nitrogen

D. phosphorus

383. What was discovered in the Yukon in 1896?

A. Dinosaur fossils

B. gold

C. oil

D. ancient tribe

384. Susan B. Antony was the first woman to be honored in this way?

A. Currency

B. medal of honor

C. building

D. law

385. Which one of these is the most densely populated city?

A. Brisbane

B. Busan

C. Mumbai

D. London

386. A Malagasy lives in which country?

A. Mali

B. Malta

C. Madagascar

D. Maldives

387. Brussels is the capital of which country?

A. Croatia

B. Greece

C. Belgium

D. Colombia

388. Where do the Grimm's fairy tales originate from?

A. Germany

B. France

C. Russia

D. Netherlands

389. What is the family name of the ruling dynasty of Monaco?

A. Gorgio

B. Giovanni

C. Grimidi

D. Grimaldi

390. What was the first source of Roman Law?

A. 12 tables

B. 13 tables

C. Pax Romana

D. mos maiorum

391. Which bone are babies born without?

A. A Rib

B. Elbow

C. Thigh Bone

D. Kneecap

392. What type of animal baby is a cria?

A. camel

B. crocodile

C. llama

D. weasel

393. Which University did Karl Marx attend in 1835?

A. London

B. Paris

C. Brussels

D. Bonn

394. When did the Cold War end?

A. 1978

B. 1989

C. 1991

D. 1994

395. Nepal is located on which continent?

A. Asia

B. Africa

C. Oceania

D. South America

396. What US state shares a border with Canada?

A. North Dakota

B. Texas

C. North Carolina

D. Nevada

397. How many U.S. Presidents were named James?

A. 3

B. 6

C. 7

D. 1

398. Which among these countries do NOT border Italy?

A. France

B. Vatican City

C. San Marino

D. Belgium

399. Name the team with the most Super Bowl appearances?

A. Buffalo Bills

B. New England Patriots

C. Dallas Cowboys

D. Pittsburgh Steelers

400. What is the function of a xylem in a plant?

A. nutrient storage

B. reproduction

C. photosynthesis

D. transport of water

401. At which hospital did the first heart transplant take place?

A. Sinai Hospital

B. Mass General

C. Barnes Hospital

D. Groote Schuur Hospital

402. Which country is closest to the Great Barrier Reef?

A. USA

B. Australia

C. India

D. Canada

403. What character did Michael J. Fox play in Back to the Future?

A. London McFly

B. Marty McFly

C. George McFly

D. Dave McFly

404. Which of the following is not a type of force?

A. acceleration

B. friction

C. gravity

D. magnetic

405. Which U.S. President was the first to ride in a Helicopter?

A. Eisenhower

B. Kennedy

C. Roosevelt

D. Truman

406. According to Greek mythology who was the first woman on earth

A. Pandora

B. Hera

C. Persephone

D. Medea

407. What was the top speed of Concorde in miles per hour?

A. 550 mph

B. 834 mph

C. 1000 mph

D. 1354 mph

408. Which country was the Caesar salad invented in?

A. Italy

B. France

C. United States

D. Mexico

409. Which English city has more miles of canals than Venice?

A. Birmingham

B. Colchester

C. Manchester

D. Coventry

410. How much DNA do humans share with bananas?

A. 0%

B. 5%

C. 50%

D. 90%

411. How long is a jiffy?

A. 22 minutes

B. One trillionth of a second

C. A quarter of a second

D. 772.4 mph

412. What is the name of the book written by Bobby Fischer?

A. My System

B. The Inner Game

C. Endgame Manual

D. My 60 Memorable Games

413. Distance is equal to speed multiplied by what?

   A. acceleration

   B. length

   C. time

   D. velocity

414. Which Disney film features the song When You Wish Upon a Star

   A. Cinderella

   B. Peter Pan

   C. Pinocchio

   D. Sleeping Beauty

415. A tick bite can make you allergic to what food?

   A. Red meat

   B. Eggs

   C. Carrots

   D. Apples

416. What is the highest grossing holiday movie of all time?

   A. The Grinch

   B. Home Alone

   C. The Night Before Christmas

   D. Christmas Witch

417. What kind of an animal is known as a horned toad?

A. A frog

B. A lizard

C. A beetle

D. A toad

418. The stirrups are located in which part of the human body?

A. ear

B. eye

C. feet

D. pelvis

419. Which building has 73 Elevators?

A. Empire State

B. Bank of America Tower

C. Chrysler Building

D. CN Tower

420. Who was the last tsar of Russia?

A. Nicholas II

B. Alexander II

C. Paul I

D. Catherine II

421. What unit of measurement is equal to 4047 square meters?

A. acre

B. hectare

C. square kilometer

D. square mile

422. How many red stripes are there on the American flag?

A. Six

B. Five

C. Seven

D. Eight

423. What is the largest planet in our solar system?

A. Saturn

B. Jupiter

C. Venus

D. Neptune

424. Which among these states is NOT in the East Coast?

A. Maine

B. Oregon

C. New York

D. Florida

425. What is a community of ants called?

A. A community

B. A collection

C. A colony

D. A collective

426. Which among these countries was NOT part of the World War I?

A. Switzerland

B. Germany

C. France

D. Japan

427. What year was the Seneca Falls Convention?

A. 1845

B. 1830

C. 1848

D. 138

428. A manatee is also known as what?

A. sea cow

B. sea elephant

C. sea horse

D. sea lion

429. Which two countries share the longest international border?

A. Canada and USA

B. Mexico and USA

C. China and Russia

D. Egypt and Libya

430. Which is the only Grand Slam tournament that is played on grass?

A. Wimbledon

B. French Open

C. US Open

D. Australian Open

431. Which of these elements is not found in ethanol (alcohol)

A. carbon

B. hydrogen

C. nitrogen

D. oxygen

432. In which country is divorce illegal?

A. Philippines

B. Iran

C. Somalia

D. Dominican Republic

433. What is the capital of Singapore?

   A. Singapore

   B. Jurong

   C. Serangoon

   D. Tampines

434. Where was the U.S. largest surrender in battle?

   A. Bataan

   B. Berlin

   C. Paris

   D. Tokyo

435. What kind of club did Cleopatra and Mark Antony form?

   A. Drinking

   B. dancing

   C. music

   D. reading

436. What is often seen as the smallest unit of memory?

   A. Gigabyte

   B. Megabyte

   C. Terabyte

   D. kilobyte

437. The Larry O'Brien Championship Trophy is awarded to:

A. The winner of the NBA Finals

B. The Eastern Conference champions

C. The Western Conference champions

D. The Central Division champions

438. The famous St. Basil's Cathedral is located in which city?

A. Copenhagen

B. Moscow

C. Madrid

D. Stockholm

439. Who said this was their finest hour?

A. Tony Blair

B. Winston Churchill

C. Woodrow Wilson

D. John Adams

440. What is the name for the group of men who elect a Pope?

A. College of Bishops

B. Meeting of Cardinals

C. Meeting of Ministers

D. College of Cardinals

441. Which city is the bike capital of the world?

A. Amsterdam

B. San Francisco

C. Budapest

D. Hong Kong

442. In Roman Myth Mars is the god of what?

A. Games

B. love

C. war

D. law

443. Where do natural pearls comes from?

A. ice

B. rock ore

C. oysters

D. whales

444. Which US state has the longest coastline?

A. Florida

B. California

C. Alabama

D. Alaska

445. Who wrote songs for The Lion King?

A. Elton John

B. Billy Joel

C. Paul McCartney

D. Stevie Wonder

446. How many time zones does Russia span?

A. 6

B. 7

C. 11

D. 15

447. Who was the first person in space?

A. Neil Armstrong

B. Yuri Gagarin

C. Alexei Leonov

D. Valentina Tereshkova

448. What is the only state that borders just one other state?

A. Maine

B. Texas

C. Montana

D. Maryland

449. It was illegal for women to wear what in 19th century Florence?

A. Buttons

B. Pants

C. Corsets

D. Pins

450. Where might you keep bees?

A. apiary

B. aquarium

C. aviary

D. vivarium

451. What is the number one seller at Walmart?

A. Toilet paper

B. Bananas

C. Socks

D. Greeting Cards

452. Which country was Joan of Arc from?

A. Russia

B. Italy

C. England

D. France

453. What country did the U.S. buy Alaska from?

A. Canada

B. Mexico

C. England

D. Russia

454. Ancient Romans boiled vinegar and what to make an energy drink?

A. Tea leaves

B. Urine

C. Compost

D. Goat poop

455. What does the gall bladder produce?

A. adrenaline

B. bile

C. gastric acid

D. insulin

456. Which country is the largest producer of chocolate?

A. Netherlands

B. United States

C. Australia

D. Germany

457. What is illegal to eat with a cherry pie in Kansas?

A. Peanut butter

B. Ice cream

C. Another pie

D. Milk

458. In which city is Jim Morrison buried?

A. London

B. Paris

C. New Orleans

D. Tokyo

459. Who was the first woman to win a Nobel Prize (1903)?

A. Bertha von Suttner

B. Jane Addams

C. Marie Curie

D. Pearl S. Buck

460. With which team has Pau Gasol won two NBA championships?

A. Chicago Bulls

B. Los Angeles Lakers

C. Memphis Grizzlies

D. San Antonio Spurs

461. Who was the first Roman emperor to claim Christianity?

A. Constantine

B. Augustus

C. Licinius

D. Dalmatius

462. In which city did the Napoleonic wars end?

A. Ligny

B. Paris

C. Waterloo

D. Wavre

463. Hinduism originated from which country?

A. Pakistan

B. India

C. Bangladesh

D. Afghanistan

464. What is the world's biggest island?

A. Borneo

B. Madagascar

C. Greenland

D. Victoria Island

465. What is the only Portuguese-speaking country in the Americas?

A. Brazil

B. Argentina

C. Uruguay

D. Central America

466. In what year were the first Air Jordan sneakers released?

A. 1979

B. 1982

C. 1987

D. 1984

467. What type of bee is always male?

A. drone

B. honey

C. queen

D. worker

468. Cirque du Soleil started in what country?

A. Canada

B. France

C. Italy

D. Mexico

469. Which country has the lowest crime rate?

A. Canada

B. Iceland

C. USA

D. Bolivia

470. What was Marilyn Monroe's natural hair color?

A. Brunette

B. Blonde

C. Black

D. Red

471. Which country is the oldest?

A. Portugal

B. New Zealand

C. Indonesia

D. Australia

472. How many teeth does an adult human typically have?

A. 20

B. 24

C. 32

D. 40

473. Who started the Russian Revolution?

A. Joseph Stalin

B. Vladimir Lenin

C. Sergei Witte

D. Peter Stolypin

474. Dutch people live in which country?

A. Georgia

B. Netherlands

C. Belgium

D. Denmark

475. Which is the brightest planet as seen from earth?

A. Jupiter

B. Mars

C. Saturn

D. Venus

476. The Statue of Liberty was given to the US by which country?

A. England

B. Canada

C. France

D. Portugal

477. What is the fastest growing plant on earth?

A. algae

B. bamboo

C. eucalyptus

D. sequoia

478. What American beer has been long promoted as the King of Beers?

A. Budweiser

B. Heineken

C. Bud Light

D. PBR

479. Which of these metals is not magnetic?

A. cobalt

B. copper

C. iron

D. nickel

480. The metamorphism of limestone forms what substance?

A. chalk

B. diamond

C. graphite

D. marble

481. What country has the most vending machines per capita?

A. South Korea

B. Japan

C. China

D. India

482. Tim Berners-Lee is credited with the invention of what?

A. computer

B. telephone

C. telescope

D. World Wide Web

483. Which of these is not a type of wild cat?

A. dingo

B. lynx

C. ocelot

D. serval

484. Which of these is a negatively charged sub-atomic particle

A. electron

B. molecule

C. neutron

D. proton

485. What type of tree grows from an acorn?

A. elm

B. fir

C. maple

D. oak

486. Hepatitis is inflammation of which organ?

A. brain

B. kidney

C. liver

D. lung

487. Who set sail on the HMS Beagle?

A. Albert Einstein

B. Charles Darwin

C. Sigmund Feud

D. James Cook

488. Which frontier did Winfield Scott fight on in the war of 1812?

A. Niagara

B. Frenchtown

C. Hampton

D. York

489. An Apgar score is given to what?

A. Graduate students

B. Health of newborns

C. Velocity of an object in a vacuum

D. Acidity in drinks

490. What does the term piano actually mean?

A. To be played softly

B. Melodious sound

C. Rising keys

D. Finger art

491. What year did the war of 1812 end?

A. 1814

B. 1812

C. 1813

D. 1815

492. Diamonds are made from which element?

A. carbon

B. platinum

C. silicon

D. silver

493. How many chambers make up the human heart?

A. 1

B. 2

C. 4

D. 6

494. Which famous landmark is visible from space?

A. The Great Wall of China

B. Taj Mahal

C. The Great Pyramids at Giza

D. Taipei 101

495. In what city did Princess Diana suffer her fatal car crash?

A. London

B. Madrid

C. Rome

D. Paris

496. What's the brightest star in the sky?

A. Vega

B. Sirius

C. Capella

D. Altair

497. Where did Barack Obama teach constitutional law?

A. University of Chicago

B. University of Illinois

C. Northwestern University

D. Loyola University

498. Which country produces the most coffee in the world?

A. Colombia

B. Vietnam

C. Mexico

D. Brazil

499. Which art movement is Salvador Dali associated with?

A. Abstract

B. Surrealism

C. Conceptualism

D. Expressionism

500. Julius Caesar was kidnapped by who in 78 BC?

A. Senate

B. Pirates

C. Enemy Nation

D. Family

Answers

ANSWERS

1. John A. Macdonald
2. Greenland
3. Proteins
4. 9,000 years
5. Vince Carter
6. Squirrels
7. Boston Celtics
8. Five
9. Japan
10. China
11. A Columella
12. Cheetah
13. Cancer
14. Amsterdam
15. Mammal
16. Erik Weisz
17. India
18. Jupiter

Answers

19. Czech Republic
20. Komodo Dragon
21. Houston Rockets
22. California
23. Bucharest
24. John Rockefeller
25. Gianni Versace
26. Skunks
27. Woodrow Wilson
28. Margaret Thatcher
29. Birds
30. Wayne Gretzky
31. Hera
32. 51
33. Elizabeth Tower
34. Daniel Keyes
35. Rand
36. Eye

Answers

37. Whitehorse

38. Bordeaux

39. Mayflies

40. Truth

41. Four

42. Precambrian

43. Finland

44. Martina Hingis

45. Barcelona

46. Odor from sweat

47. Kosmoceratops

48. The Arctic

49. Hamlet

50. Joe DiMaggio

51. History

52. Fiji

53. 38 minutes

54. Purple

ANSWERS

55. Peter

56. Afghanistan

57. Mars

58. GPS

59. Nepal

60. A farrier

61. Montreal

62. A kid

63. Benjamin Franklin

64. Doha

65. Occipital lobe

66. Flamingos

67. Distance

68. Mandarin

69. Troposphere

70. Evolution

71. Mediterranean Sea

72. Greek. Egyptian

ANSWERS

73. Chinese

74. Peter III

75. Africa

76. Saturn and Jupiter

77. Saigon

78. Energy

79. Philippines

80. Kentucky

81. Iran

82. Henry VIII

83. Three

84. South Dakota

85. Toronto

86. 95

87. Pimento

88. Roosevelt

89. Lincoln

90. Tea

Answers

91. Nirvana
92. Goering
93. Joe DiMaggio
94. Pigs
95. Rhode Island
96. Peach
97. Toxic
98. Fruit flies
99. Green
100. Garbanzo
101. Vermeer
102. India
103. Carbon dioxide
104. Afghanistan
105. 50
106. 12
107. Vatican City
108. Protestant Reformation

Answers

109. Darwin

110. Hydrogen

111. Colorado River

112. Baltimore Ravens

113. Nile

114. Ice

115. Beagle

116. Fried Chicken

117. Green

118. Vitamin A

119. Thailand

120. Chennai

121. Evaporation

122. Truman Capote

123. Black

124. Portugal

125. California

126. Centillion

Answers

127. E

128.. A bishop

129. Gaul

130. Eel

131. Athens

132. Cuba

133. Physics

134. Cambodia

135. Ohio

136. Ming

137. France

138. Justin Rolland

139. Big Toe

140. LIV

141. Euro

142. George

143. Alexander Hamilton

144. Pakistan

ANSWERS

145. New Zealand

146. Howard Carter

147. Bavarian Motor Works

148. Timor-Leste

149. March 15th

150. China

151. 2007

152. Abortion

153. Splash Brothers

154. Saint

155. Switzerland

156. Famine

157. Arnold Palmer

158. Leonardo da Vinci

159. Canberra

160. Australia

161. Vatican City

162. Oxygen

ANSWERS

163. Henry VII

164. Australia

165. Alicia Silverstone

166. UAE

167. Ag

168. Deliver mail

169. Wandering Albatross

170. 1849

171. Iceland

172. 7

173. The Murray River

174. Sugars

175. Facial cheek

176. Lithosphere

177. To hold flowers

178. World War 1

179. Sun

180. 55 miles

ANSWERS

181. Germany

182. Last player to play without a helmet

183. X-ray Crystallography

184. Tears

185. Oldest player to score 40+ points in a game

186. Esperanto

187. China

188. Christmas Tree Farm

189. China and India

190. 1989

191. China

192. Georgia

193. The Bleeding tooth fungus

194. France

195. Art

196. Lead

197. 1867

198. Hydrogen

ANSWERS

199. Telephone

200. 7

201. New York

202. Sri Lanka

203. Pineal gland

204. Michelangelo

205. 7

206. Armpit

207. Jane Austen

208. Tennis court

209. Ted Williams

210. Leonardo da Vinci

211. It changed color

212. France

213. Chile

214. USA

215. Norma Jeane

216. Ganymede (Jupiter)

Answers

217. 4

218. Twice cooked

219. Alexander Hamilton

220. Kenya

221. Three

222. Femur

223. Kursk

224. The Dakota Building

225. Teacher

226. 1973

227. Gary Player

228. Neon

229. Italy

230. Julius Caesar

231. Restricted

232. Bones

233. Amsterdam

234. Luxembourg

ANSWERS

235. A bird

236. Robert Zimmerman

237. New Zealand

238. 3

239. New Mexico

240. 2

241. Head injury

242. Canada

243. Mosquito

244. Seoul

245. Lawrence Peter Berra

246. His shadow

247. 5

248. Tree-ring dating

249. Orange

250. Atlanta

251. 8 minutes

252. Ballet

ANSWERS

253. China

254. Sweden

255. Liberia

256. Best left-handed pitcher

257. Israel

258. Venus

259. Commodus

260. Haiti

261. Thailand

262. Papua New Guinea

263. Arizona and Hawaii

264. Toronto

265. Beetle

266. Harper Lee

267. Helsinki

268. Resistance

269. A Rabbit

270. Amp

Answers

271. Bicycle

272. River Seine

273. Hawaii

274. Prius

275. Pumice

276. 24

277. Solid State Drive

278. Washington D.C.

279. 3

280. Talladega Superspeedway

281. Georgia

282. USA

283. Caligula

284. Tooth Enamel

285. Mary Shelley

286. Benjamin Franklin

287. Mr. Red

288. Gary Cooper

ANSWERS

289. San Francisco

290. Palace

291. Paris

292. 1 kilogram

293. Charles Lindbergh

294. The Crimean War

295. 14

296. Vienna

297. Mona Lisa

298. Aristotle

299. Gary Larson

300. Aorta

301. England

302. Taiwan

303. Talc

304. Albany

305. Knot

306. Moby Dick

Answers

307. 118

308. Vatican City

309. Violet

310. Subatomic particle

311. Hurricanes

312. Aluminum

313. Matt Groening

314. China

315. Martin Luther

316. Code of Ur-Nammu

317. Alternating current

318. 9

319. South Africa

320. Bakery

321. New Jersey

322. North Atlantic

323. Jules Verne

324.. LeBron James

Answers

325. Bedwetting
326. England
327. Poland
328. Yen
329. Asuncion
330. Samuel Adams
331. A spider
332. Lou Gehrig
333. A stag
334. Australia
335. The Netherlands
336. Scotland
337. Spiciness
338. Wings
339. Turkeys
340. Turkey
341. The Spanish Civil War
342. Kazakhstan

Answers

343. 1920

344. Vinegar

345. Mali

346. 101

347. Cats

348. Peru

349. Spain

350. Elizabeth

351. Nevis

352. England

353. Henry Ford

354. 0

355. USA

356. League of Nations

357. Sputnik I

358. Edward Smith

359. Tanzania

360. Round

Answers

361. James VI

362. Naked

363. A type of sandstorm

364. Indonesia

365. Bucephalus

366. Soviet Union

367. Hummingbird

368. Seattle

369. Japan

370. 1969

371. 1 mile

372. Mormonism

373. London

374. Strengths

375. The Great Dane

376. Africa

377. Plant tissue

378. The moon

ANSWERS

379. Teddy Roosevelt

380. FBI

381. Beheaded

382. Calcium

383. Gold

384. Currency

385. Mumbai

386. Madagascar

387. Belgium

388. Germany

389. Grimaldi

390. 12 tables

391. Kneecap

392. Llama

393. Bonn

394. 1989

395. Asia

396. North Dakota

Answers

397. 6

398. Belgium

399. New England Patriots

400. Transport of water

401. Groote Schuur Hospital

402. Australia

403. Marty McFly

404. Acceleration

405. Eisenhower

406. Pandora

407. 1354 mph

408. Mexico

409. Birmingham

410. 50%

411. One trillionth of a second

412. My 60 Memorable Games

413. Time

414. Pinocchio

Answers

415. Red meat

416. Home Alone

417. A lizard

418. Ear

419. Empire State

420. Nicholas II

421. Acre

422. Seven

423. Jupiter

424. Oregon

425. A colony

426. Switzerland

427. 1848

428. Sea cow

429. Canada and the USA

430. Wimbledon

431. Nitrogen

432. Philippines

ANSWERS

433. Singapore

434. Bataan

435. Drinking

436. Kilobyte

437. The winner of the NBA Finals

438. Moscow

439. Winston Churchill

440. College of Cardinals

441. Amsterdam

442. War

443. Oysters

444. Alaska

445. Elton John

446. 11

447. Yuri Gagarin

448. Maine

449. Buttons

450. Apiary

Answers

451. Bananas
452. France
453. Russia
454. Goat Poop
455. Bile
456. Germany
457. Ice cream
458. Paris
459. Marie Curie
460. Los Angeles Lakers
461. Constantine
462. Waterloo
463. Pakistan
464. Greenland
465. Brazil
466. 1984
467. Drone
468. Canada

Answers

469. Iceland

470. Red

471. Portugal

472. 32

473. Vladimir Lenin

474. Netherlands

475. Venus

476. France

477. Bamboo

478. Budweiser

479. Copper

480. Marble

481. Japan

482. World Wide Web

483. Dingo

484. Electron

485. Oak

486. Liver

Answers

487. Charles Darwin

488. Niagara

489. Health of newborns

490. To be played softly

491. 1815

492. Carbon

493. 4

494. The Great Pyramids at Giza

495. Paris

496. Sirius

497. University of Chicago

498. Brazil

499. Surrealism

500. Pirates

Made in United States
North Haven, CT
24 November 2023

44475639R00089